DILEMMAS IN
DEMOCRACY

Voter Disenfranchisement

Derek Miller

Cavendish
Square

New York

Library of Congress Cataloging-in-Publication Data

Names: Miller, Derek.
Title: Voter disenfranchisement / Derek Miller.
Description: New York : Cavendish Square Publishing, 2020. | Series:
Dilemmas in democracy | Includes glossary and index.
Identifiers: ISBN 9781502645098 (pbk.) | ISBN 9781502645104
(library bound) | ISBN 9781502645111 (ebook)
Subjects: LCSH: Suffrage--United States--Juvenile literature. | Voting--United States--Juvenile literature. |
Elections--United States--Juvenile literature. | Political rights, Loss of--United States--Juvenile literature.
Classification: LCC JK1846.M555 2020 | DDC 303.6/20973--dc23

Editorial Director: David McNamara
Editor: Caitlyn Miller
Copy Editor: Alex Tessman
Associate Art Director: Alan Sliwinski
Designer: Christina Shults
Production Coordinator: Karol Szymczuk
Photo Research: J8 Media

The photographs in this book are used by permission and through the courtesy of:
Cover Richard Levine/Alamy Stock Photo; background (and used throughout the book) Artist Elizaveta/
Shutterstock.com; p. 4 Gregory Rec/Portland Press Herald/Getty Images; p. 10 Elijah Nouvelage/
Bloomberg via Getty Images; p. 11 Chris Maddaloni/CQ Roll Call/Getty Images; p. 12 Silus Grok
from Salt Lake City, Utah, USA/Wikimedia Commons/File:Precinct Map (291775064).jpg/CC BY
SA 2.0; p. 15 Visions of America/UIG/Getty Images; p. 18 Mandel Ngan/AFP/Getty Images; p. 21 Jeff
Kowalsky/AFP/Getty Images; p. 22 Mark Ralston/AFP/Getty Images; p. 24 Universal History Archive/
Getty Images; p. 27 Ken Florey Suffrage Collection/Gado/Getty Images; p. 30-31 Everett Historical/
Shutterstock.com; p. 32 Popperfoto/Getty Images; p. 40-41 Sean Pavone/Shutterstock.com; p. 42
Encyclopedia Britannica/UIG/Getty Images; p. 44 Sia Kambou/AFP/Getty Images; p. 46-47 Chris Wattie/
Reuters/Newscom; p. 49 Ilia Yemovich/Getty Images; p. 51 Per-Anders Pettersson/Getty Images; p.
52 Mehedi Hasan/NurPhoto via Getty Images; p. 54 PEW Research Center; p. 57 AFP/Getty Images;
p. 58 Rhona Wise/AFP/Getty Images; p. 61 Brendan Hoffman/Getty Images; p. 63 Charles Bonnay/
The LIFE Images Collection/Getty Images; p. 64-65 Robert W. Kelley/The LIFE Picture Collection/
Getty Images; p. 67 Antonio Guillem/Shutterstock.com; p. 68-69 AAraujo/Shutterstock.com.

Printed in the United States of America

CONTENTS

CHAPTER 1

What Is Voter Disenfranchisement?

Few rights are as important as the right to vote. The ability of the people to choose their leaders is the foundation of democracy, and voting is how people make that choice. Taking away someone's right to vote silences their voice. Someone who cannot vote has no say in who leads the country. They cannot make their wishes known, and therefore, the government no longer represents them. As a result, the issues of who can vote and who should have their right to vote taken away are some of the most important questions that a democracy faces.

Disenfranchisement

When someone's right to vote is taken away, it is called disenfranchisement. Sometimes, disenfranchisement is a punishment. In many US states, people convicted of serious crimes—felonies—are disenfranchised for a time by law. They

Opposite: A woman in Maine exercises her right to vote during the 2014 elections.

may not be allowed to vote in prison, after being released, or even for the rest of their lives in the strictest states.

Felony disenfranchisement is legal in the United States. However, it is still controversial. Many people believe that it violates the rights of people convicted of felonies. On the other hand, supporters say that people convicted of serious crimes should not have the right to vote because of their past choices.

Often, disenfranchisement is not as straightforward as felony disenfranchisement. Instead of being a punishment, disenfranchisement is sometimes carried out through voting restriction laws or practices. Voting restriction laws make it more difficult to vote. Broadly speaking, voting restriction laws are legal when they do not intend to disenfranchise anyone. They are illegal when they intend to disenfranchise specific groups of people, like minority or elderly voters.

The question of whether voting restriction laws disenfranchise people is a divisive one. It is an ongoing debate both in Washington, DC, and in state governments across the country. Since 2013, many states have passed voting restriction laws. Supporters say they make voter fraud less likely. (Voter fraud occurs when votes are cast illegally by someone who does not have the right to vote or when someone casts more than one vote.) Opponents say voting restriction laws disenfranchise people, often minority voters.

The judicial system has weighed in on some of these laws. Laws judged to disenfranchise minority voters have been struck down by courts, while other voting restrictions have been upheld in court. Judges look at the details and effects of laws before deciding if they are appropriate.

How Disenfranchisement Works

Many different laws and practices can result in disenfranchisement. Practices that make it difficult or time-consuming to cast a ballot may rise to the level of disenfranchisement. Difficulty in casting a ballot is especially concerning when it affects certain voters more than others.

Voters from rural areas and minority neighborhoods as well as voters with disabilities and elderly voters sometimes face more difficulty when casting a ballot. Whether this qualifies as disenfranchisement is somewhat of a political question. Supporters of the current system argue that difficulty voting is an accidental result of current laws and practices. Critics argue that in some cases laws and practices are meant to silence voters. When many people are disenfranchised, it is called voter suppression.

We will now look at the most common practices and laws that critics say disenfranchise certain voters. These issues affect particular states and polling districts more than others. Ongoing court cases and political debates address whether these specific state and local practices should be allowed or if they disenfranchise too many voters.

Long Waits at the Polls

Voters are sometimes forced to wait hours before casting their vote. This issue raises worries about disenfranchisement, especially when wait times are only long in some areas. In the 2018 elections, many different states and districts struggled to allow voters to cast their ballot in a reasonable amount of time. Long wait times can result from any number of issues: malfunctioning voting machines, a lack of poll workers, higher turnout than expected, or poor management.

The Universal Declaration of Human Rights

Not everyone in the world has the right to vote. Many people live in countries where they are not allowed to express themselves politically. There may not be elections at all, or there may be elections, but citizens face imprisonment or death if they vote against the government.

According to the Democracy Index, which is compiled by a well-respected analysis group, 76 of the 167 world countries studied are democracies. About 49.3 percent of the world's population lives in one of these democratic countries. The remainder live in countries that are not democracies. They may have the right to vote in elections, but the elections are not free. Opponents to the ruling party may not be allowed to run, or the result of the election may be predetermined.

Despite the current state of affairs, taking part in a free and democratic government is a human right. Human rights are fundamental rights that all human beings have. Many international agreements and treaties describe the human rights that countries around the world agree on. One of the most important of these documents is the Universal Declaration of Human Rights. It was adopted by the United Nations (UN), an organization made up of the countries of the world, in 1948.

The Universal Declaration of Human Rights spells out the rights that all human beings ought to have no matter where they live. These include the rights to life, marriage, and property ownership. Other human rights ban practices like slavery and torture. Article 21 of the Universal Declaration of Human Rights outlines a person's right to take part in government:

1. *Everyone has the right to take part in the government of his country, directly or through freely chosen representatives.*

2. *Everyone has the right of equal access to public service in his country.*

3. *The will of the people shall be the basis of the authority of government; this will shall be expressed in periodic and genuine elections which shall be by universal and equal suffrage and shall be held by secret vote or by equivalent free voting procedures.*

The idea of "universal and equal suffrage" is incompatible with most forms of disenfranchisement, considering suffrage is the right to vote. However, the Universal Declaration of Human Rights is not legally binding in the United States. It is up the American government—and the governments of other countries—to ensure that human rights are protected.

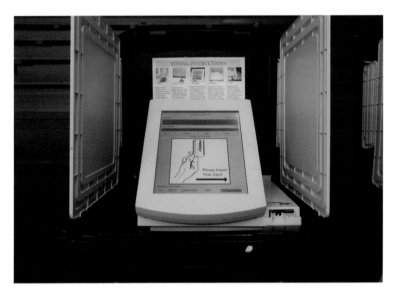

Many districts use electronic voting machines. Malfunctioning machines sometimes cause long wait times at the polls.

South Carolina was one state that had many cases of long wait times in 2018. Melanie Taylor, a resident of Charleston, tried to vote at 7:15 in the morning, but when she arrived, the line was outside of the building. After forty-five minutes of waiting, she had to give up so that she could make it to work. Taylor later spoke about her experience to journalist Isaac Arnsdorf at *ProPublica*: "It felt like a type of disenfranchisement, even though there wasn't any violation of voting rights. The wait has been all day three hours or more, which is ridiculous."

Long wait times disproportionately (or unequally) affect low-income voters. Low-income voters are more likely to work jobs with inflexible hours. They are less likely to be able to take off half a day or rearrange their work schedule to vote. Meanwhile, office workers are much more likely to be able to change their hours so that

Long lines at polling stations can discourage people from voting, especially if they do not have much time. Here, voters wait to cast their ballot in Washington, DC.

they can vote. The disproportionate affect of long wait times raises concerns that such wait times disenfranchise low-income voters.

Additionally, wait times may be longer in low-income or minority neighborhoods. When resources are distributed, they may receive fewer voting machines or poll workers. Longer wait times in certain neighborhoods can disenfranchise residents of those areas.

Limiting Where to Vote

In addition to wait times, the location of polling places can also disenfranchise voters. Ideally, voters can easily reach a polling place to cast their ballot. However, some states are closing polling places. State governments justify these closures by saying that they save

Cities are divided into precincts—or voting districts. Residents of precincts are assigned a polling place where they can cast their ballot. This map shows Salt Lake City's precincts.

money, but it also makes it more difficult for voters to cast their ballot. Reducing the number of polling places especially hurts voters who do not own a car or who live in rural areas with poor public transportation.

Georgia made headlines recently for closing polling places. Between 2012 and 2018, almost 8 percent of the state's polling places were closed, meaning many voters had to travel farther to vote. Additionally, many of the closures occurred in areas with large numbers of African Americans. For instance, in Randolph County, which is 61 percent African American, there were plans to close seven of the nine polling places. A public outcry stopped the plans, but critics say polling places are often closed in minority counties and neighborhoods.

The state government defended these decisions by saying that they were based on how many ballots were cast at a location. Critics argued it was a troubling choice in a state that used to disenfranchise African Americans through racist laws. Furthermore, Republican officials were the ones responsible for picking which polling places should close, and most African Americans vote for Democrats over Republicans.

Voter Purges

Voter purges occur when people are deleted from voting rolls in large numbers. There is an open debate about classifying voter purges as disenfranchisement. State government justify purges by saying that purges help them keep voting rolls up-to-date. Opponents say that voter purges affect minority groups far more than other voters and result in their disenfranchisement.

The Supreme Court recently heard a case called *Husted v. Randolph Institute* about a voter purge in Ohio. The Ohio purge deleted the names of people who had not voted in the past two years, not returned a card mailed to them, and then once again not voted for four years. The mailing of the card was important because it is against the law for states to delete names from voting rolls simply because those people have not voted recently. In a close decision, five Supreme Court justices found that the purge was legal. They narrowly beat out the four justices who thought it was illegal.

Supreme Court Justice Sonia Sotomayor was one justice who argued the purge was illegal. She pointed to the fact that it unequally affected "minority, low-income, disabled, and veteran voters." Voter purges are much more likely to delete the names of people who do not speak English at home, cannot read well, or cannot vote regularly because their work schedule is inflexible. Whether or not this makes purges illegal is still a heated topic.

Voter ID Laws

Voter ID laws are some of the most common voting restrictions enacted in recent years. These laws require voters to carry specific identification cards to the polls when they vote. This is meant to prevent people from casting a ballot with another person's name on it, as well as some other types of voter fraud. Unfortunately, many people who have the right to vote do not have the correct identification cards. This is a problem that affects poor, elderly, and minority voters most often. As a result, some voters are disenfranchised by voter ID laws.

The main question about voter ID laws is if this disenfranchisement is worth it because it prevents some cases of voter fraud. Critics say it is not. In-person voter fraud is extremely rare, while voters who do not have a driver's license or other photo ID are relatively common. Supporters of voter ID laws say all voters should be capable of getting photo ID if they want to vote.

One state that passed a voter ID law in the last ten years is Wisconsin. The 2011 law requires all voters to bring one of seven types of identification with them to vote. When ballots were cast in the 2016 election, an estimated three hundred thousand voters did not have one of these forms of ID.

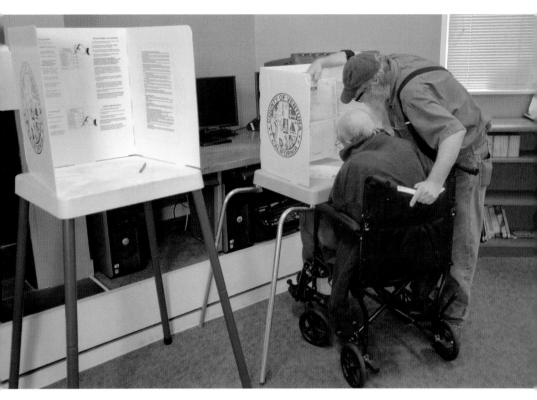

Uncertainty about voting requirements and long wait times can affect elderly and disabled voters more than others.

One such voter was thirty-year-old Navy veteran Sean Reynolds. He was turned away from the polls because he brought an out-of-state driver's license from Illinois. Reynolds later told the *Wisconsin State Journal* how the experience made him feel: "Coming home [from the military] and being denied the right to vote because I didn't have a specific driver's license is very frustrating. I was a little incredulous that they wouldn't accept another state's driver's license. I didn't understand why it was not a valid form of ID."

Reynold's story is not unique. Many voters have reported being unable to cast ballots because of issues they did not know about with their identification cards. Typically, voters are given a handful of days to bring back the correct identification so that their vote can be cast. However, those who work and cannot get time off, like Reynolds, found themselves unable to vote at all.

Is Disenfranchisement Legal?

The legality of laws and practices that disenfranchise voters are at the center of raging debates. Disenfranchisement is not a simple issue with clear answers. It is useful to look at past court decisions related to disenfranchisement since it is the courts that ultimately decide if a law is allowed. Nonetheless, different judges will often arrive at a different conclusion about the same law. The Supreme Court has the ultimate say about a law, but they do not agree to hear every court case. A look at similar cases heard by the Supreme Court is informative, but small differences between laws mean that one law is struck down while a nearly identical law is upheld.

The most straightforward judgment related to disenfranchisement is that felony disenfranchisement is allowed. Many courts have decided this, and that decision is based in large part on the Fourteenth Amendment to the Constitution. The Constitution is the highest law of the land that all other laws must not contradict. If a law does contradict the Constitution, courts can rule it unconstitutional and overturn it. The Fourteenth Amendment says that states may be punished for taking away the right to vote from men over the age of twenty-one "except for participation in

Transgender Voters and Voter ID Laws

Voter ID laws can result in the disenfranchisement of many different groups of people. One group that is affected by voter ID laws is the transgender community. At least a quarter of transgender voters have an ID that does not accurately reflect their gender. This can lead to problems when they try to vote in states that have passed voter ID laws.

A 2016 report by the Williams Institute warns that voter ID laws could disenfranchise tens of thousands of transgender voters across the country. It is a difficult and costly process to try to change the gender listed on a person's identification. When transgender people present identification that does not accurately reflect their gender, harassment and even violence can result. It is unclear how poll workers will treat transgender voters or if poll workers will consider their identification valid if the gender is inaccurate.

NBC News spoke to one transgender voter, Oliver, who reported that he had been made to wait approximately an hour in the 2014 election when his identification did not accurately reflect his gender. After insisting that he had the right to vote, he was eventually allowed to, but he told *NBC News* he found the situation humiliating.

Currently, voter ID laws threaten to disenfranchise many transgender voters. Transgender voters are uniquely affected by these new laws and are much more likely to have negative experiences at polling places as a result.

The Supreme Court decides whether laws are constitutional, including laws about voting. The court doesn't agree to hear all cases, however.

rebellion, or other crime." Courts have decided that this line justifies felony disenfranchisement as constitutional.

Many other types of disenfranchisement are unconstitutional. Constitutional amendments forbid states from disenfranchising voters on account of their race, sex, or age (once they turn eighteen). The Twenty-Fourth Amendment even forbids states from requiring voters to pay a tax to cast their ballot. (Such poll taxes were used to disenfranchise low-income and minority voters in the past.) Federal laws—passed by Congress—forbid other practices that were historically used to disenfranchise voters. One example is the outlawing of voter purges based solely on the fact that a person did not cast their ballot in a previous election.

Outside of clear cases of disenfranchisement based on issues like race, the legality of voting restriction laws tends to be controversial. There are two major competing ideas. On the one hand, states have the right to organize elections within the bounds of the law. States regulate elections to reduce voter fraud, keep their costs down, and keep voter rolls up-to-date by deleting names of people who have died or moved. On the other hand, these state practices should not be permitted to disenfranchise large numbers of voters without cause. Additionally, state laws should not disproportionately disenfranchise voters of a certain race, sex, or age since that is unconstitutional. The current debate over practices like closing polling places and new voter ID laws focus on these issues. Much of the debate centers on data about how common election fraud is and how many people specific state laws disenfranchise. These practical questions are important when weighing the benefit—or harm—of a law.

The Consequences of Disenfranchisement

When disenfranchisement occurs, it has many negative effects. On the individual level, it violates a person's rights. When the government takes away a person's right to vote without reason, it is a great injustice. Victims of this injustice may lose faith that their government is working for them.

For the country as a whole, disenfranchisement is also a serious problem. The disenfranchisement of minority voters leads to many negative outcomes. It skews the results of elections and makes it so that politicians do not actually represent the people, creating a disconnect between the government and the people that it ought to represent. This disconnect can have real consequences. Schools and public services in minority neighborhoods receive less funding when their residents lose their right to vote.

The United States has been slowly expanding the right to vote and reducing these negative consequences throughout its history. However, according to critics, a flurry of new voting restriction laws in recent years is threatening that progress. It is up to Americans to decide if these new laws are justified or threaten democracy. Through making our voices heard, we can shape the way that the government handles the right to vote.

When people are disenfranchised, they cannot vote, and they lose faith in the government.

CHAPTER 2

Voter Disenfranchisement in America

Modern American debates about disenfranchisement are tightly tied to past instances of disenfranchisement. Throughout most of American history, the franchise—or right to vote—has not been universal. Women, men without land, African Americans, and other minorities have all gone without the right to vote. Gradually, the franchise was extended to these groups, but it was not always a simple process. Even after gaining the right to vote in amendments to the Constitution, African Americans were systematically disenfranchised for nearly a century. The laws and constitutional amendments that tried to limit racist practices of disenfranchisement are still relevant. Today, they are at the center of the debate about voter ID laws and unequal access to polls.

Opposite: Many states rely on paper ballots rather than electronic voting machines.

Most Americans did not have the right to vote when George Washington was elected as the nation's first president.

Voting in Early America

As the foundation of the American government, the most important document in the United States is the Constitution. Any law that contradicts it is invalid. The Constitution spells out how the federal government in Washington, DC, is organized and what powers the president, Congress, and judges have. However, the Constitution is a short document, and much of the day-to-day running of the country is governed by later laws, not the Constitution.

When the Constitution was written in 1787, it did not specify who could vote in elections. This decision was left to individual states. At that time, suffrage was not seen as a universal right of all human beings, as it is regarded today. For decades in early America, suffrage was restricted to white men over the age of twenty-one who owned property. Men without property, women, African Americans (free or enslaved), Native Americans, and adults under the age of twenty-one were generally not allowed to vote, although exact laws varied by state.

The restrictions that prevented poor white men from voting were the first to be abolished. Change was carried out state by state. By the 1850s, most voting restrictions based on property or wealth had been done away with. Nonetheless, the franchise was restricted to white men for many more years.

Women's Right to Vote

In the 1840s, the women's suffrage movement began to gain momentum in the United States. Members of the movement, called suffragists, called for the right to vote to be extended to women. They participated in marches in cities around the country and tried to convince lawmakers to support their efforts.

The Reconstruction Amendments

During Reconstruction, three constitutional amendments were passed to protect the rights of African Americans. The Thirteenth Amendment abolished slavery. The Fourteenth Amendment granted citizenship to people born in the United States, ensuring that newly freed slaves were citizens. It also gave all people "equal protection under the law." This phrase prevented states from discriminating against black people, but its exact meaning has changed over time. The Supreme Court once used it to justify racial segregation in 1896 before using the same phrase to overturn segregation in public schools in 1954.

The Fifteenth Amendment states, "The right of citizens of the United States to vote shall not be denied or abridged by the United States or by any State on account of race, color, or previous condition of servitude." It was meant to prevent Southern states from disenfranchising African Americans. In practice, the Fifteenth Amendment failed to do so for nearly a century between its ratification in 1870 and the end of the civil rights movement in the mid-1960s. Nonetheless, the Reconstruction Amendments were an important step forward in American history and struck a blow against racial injustice.

Suffragists demonstrate for the right to vote in 1900.

Some suffragists even voted and tried to get courts to hear their case when they were arrested for doing so, hoping the courts would decide they had the right to vote. This strategy failed when the Supreme Court unanimously ruled in 1875 that women did not have the right to vote. Nevertheless, the suffragists carried on, and eventually their efforts paid off. In 1920, the Nineteenth Amendment was passed. It forbids the federal government and states from denying a person's right to vote based on their sex.

African Americans and Disenfranchisement

At the same time as the women's suffrage movement, African Americans were also looking for suffrage. Even while slavery existed in the South, free blacks in the North were fighting for the right to vote. In fact, suffragists and important African American leaders often joined forces in their campaigns to extend the franchise.

When the United States first became a country, free African Americans in many states in the North had the right to vote—even though slavery was still practiced in these states. Gradually, many Northern states both took away the right to vote from free blacks and abolished slavery. Slavery became a controversial issue that divided free states in the North and slave states in the South. While Northern states turned against slavery, few Northerners supported equal rights for African Americans. Despite the efforts of African American campaigners for the right to vote, sweeping change only came with the end of the Civil War.

Reconstruction

The period after the Civil War is known as Reconstruction. Confederate states could rejoin the Union on the condition that they ratified three constitutional amendments guaranteeing the rights of African Americans. There was a national debate over how the South should be treated given the bloody war that many Northerners blamed them for starting.

President Andrew Johnson wanted to treat the South kindly. He thought this would help heal the nation. Although slavery was abolished by the Thirteenth Amendment, Johnson was happy to let the same political class who had owned slaves continue to run

Southern states. State governments in the South soon found ways to take rights away from recently freed African Americans with no opposition from Johnson.

However, Congress was controlled by the Radical Republicans. They wanted to punish the South and guarantee that former slaves kept their newfound freedom. To do this, they put the South under military occupation. Soldiers ensured that African Americans could vote without fear of violence. Their efforts were so successful that African Americans across the South soon held political offices, but military occupation could not last. In 1877, soldiers withdrew from the South, and the new political rights of African Americans across the South were soon taken away.

Jim Crow

Between 1877 and the mid-1960s, Southern states systematically stripped away the rights of African Americans. This system of racial segregation became known as Jim Crow. Blacks and whites went to different schools and hospitals. While these services were supposed to be equal, they were not. Public services for African Americans were given a fraction of the money that public services for whites received. Often, black people could not live in the same neighborhoods as white people. Even the US military was segregated according to race, with black and white soldiers serving in separate units.

A cornerstone of Jim Crow was the disenfranchisement of African Americans across the South. Different laws and practices were used to prevent them from voting. As a result, African Americans were often not represented in state government or in Washington, DC. Their anger at the injustice of Jim Crow went unvoiced in the halls of power.

Forbidden from entering white businesses during the Jim Crow era, African Americans opened their own.

Violence at the Polls

Violence was one way that African Americans were disenfranchised during Jim Crow. Black people who went to the polls to vote were harassed, assaulted, and even killed. Lynchings took place across the South. Gangs of white people would kill African Americans who they thought insulted whites or committed a crime. Lynchings were often done in public and not even hidden from the police, who did not hold lynch mobs accountable. Sometimes, African Americans who tried to vote were targeted. The atmosphere of

Members of the Ku Klux Klan wear white robes and hoods at a 1956 meeting.

terror that the public lynchings of African Americans caused also prevented many black people from even trying to vote.

Terrorist white supremacist groups like the Ku Klux Klan (KKK) contributed to the violence. Members believed that whites were superior to blacks and that African Americans should be oppressed through violence and terror. During some periods, KKK members included US congressmen and other prominent politicians. The deep-seated racism of the times allowed people to be public in their support of the violent movement.

Poll Taxes

Voters in some states were required to pay a poll tax to cast their ballot. The amount was enough that people with little means could not afford to pay it. This included most African Americans in the South, who were only recently freed from slavery. Their descendants were also impoverished due to the segregation of schools and discrimination.

Unlike most other laws that disenfranchised African Americans, poll taxes also disenfranchised many low-income white voters. They affected all races equally, though their usual purpose was to prevent African Americans from voting.

Voting Restrictions and Grandfather Clauses

Before the civil rights movement, a complex system of laws and rules about voting often disenfranchised African Americans. States passed laws that greatly restricted the franchise, such as literacy and property tests. Voters were required to demonstrate reading skills or wealth far beyond the reach of many Americans at the time. African Americans were especially hit hard because of the poor public education available to them and a complete lack of family wealth since many had been enslaved.

Additionally, many of these harsh voting restrictions were coupled with grandfather clauses. To avoid literacy and property tests, voters could simply show that their grandfather had voted. As a result, white voters who could not pass the tests could still vote, while African Americans could not since their grandparents had not been allowed to vote in the past. In theory, these laws treated all races equally, but in practice they were meant to disenfranchise African Americans while allowing white voters to cast their ballot.

The Civil Rights Movement

Throughout the Jim Crow era, African Americans challenged the unjust laws that oppressed them. Often, they used the courts to try to have unjust laws overturned. Sometimes, taking a case before a judge did not lead to the expected result. One activist, Homer Plessy, sat in a train car for whites in Louisiana. When he was arrested for not sitting in the "colored" train car, he filed a lawsuit hoping that courts would side with him. Instead, in 1896, the case reached the Supreme Court, and it ruled that segregation was legal so long as facilities were "separate but equal." It was a devastating blow to those fighting for justice, and a stain on American history.

In the 1950s, activists began using new strategies instead of bringing lawsuits and talking to lawmakers. They began to take action against unjust practices. When bus companies forced black people to sit in the back of the bus, they boycotted the buses. When restaurants for "whites only" refused to serve them, African American activists had sit-ins, refusing to leave despite harassment. When they were disenfranchised across entire states, they marched peacefully through state capitals in the face of police brutality and mass arrests. This mass movement was called the civil rights movement. It was led by famous figures like Dr. Martin Luther King Jr., who refused to accept the injustices of the period.

The Voting Rights Act

The civil rights movement ended in the mid-1960s when many new laws were passed that made racial discrimination illegal. The last one was the Civil Rights Act of 1968, or Fair Housing Act, which made it illegal for landlords to discriminate against renters based on their "race, color, religion, or national origin."

The earlier Voting Rights Act of 1965 was meant to end the practice of disenfranchising African Americans across the South. It was a major victory for the civil rights movement, and it remains an important law today. Courts still refer to it in cases regarding voter ID laws and other voting restrictions.

The Voting Rights Act contains many provisions to protect minority voters. It outlawed many practices of Jim Crow, such as literacy tests. In communities where languages other than English are widely used, it requires bilingual ballots. One of the most important requirements of the law is Section 5. This section requires some state and local governments to get approval from the federal government or courts before changing any voting laws. Which states need pre-approval to change voting laws was determined by a formula that looked at issues like what percentage of people were registered to vote and if there were any tests during voter registration.

In 2013, the Supreme Court ruled in *Shelby County v. Holder* that the formula used in Section 5 was outdated. As a result, no state or local government needs to seek pre-approval to change voting laws. If Congress updates Section 5, it will come into force once again. As of early 2019, Congress has not reached an agreement to update the formula.

Since *Shelby County v. Holder*, many states that used to be covered by Section 5 have passed a flurry of voting restriction laws and closed polling places. According to the *New York Times*, Alabama is one such state that has made it harder for minority voters to cast a ballot since 2013. In Alabama, polling places were closed, with many of the closures in minority neighborhoods. A voter photo-ID law was passed. The next year, driver's license offices, where photo IDs can be acquired, were closed across the state, mostly in minority areas. Critics believe these new voting restrictions amount to a new era of disenfranchisement.

Voter ID Laws

Supporters of measures like the voter ID law in Alabama argue that they prevent voter fraud. In particular, voter ID laws prevent one type of fraud: impersonation of a registered voter at a polling place. Critics argue that while this may be true, this type of voter fraud is extraordinarily rare.

Courts have generally agreed that voter impersonation is rare, but voter ID laws are still constitutional. The 2008 Supreme Court decision *Crawford v. Marion County Election Board* upheld an Indiana voter ID law. The decision noted that "the record contains no evidence of [impersonation] fraud actually occurring in Indiana at any time in its history." Nonetheless, the decision states, "the risk of voter fraud is real," and the voter ID law is a "limited burden" on voters. As a result, the law was constitutional.

Some voter ID laws have not fared so well. North Carolina passed a strict voter ID law in 2013. The state was soon taken to court by activists who said the purpose of the law was to disenfranchise minorities. It was claimed that state lawmakers crafted a bill using voter data to target African Americans and prevent them from voting. Requirements like showing photo ID, not being able to register and vote on the same day, and having to vote in a specific precinct affected African Americans more than white voters, according to state data. In this case, a federal court agreed and tossed out the voter ID law. In the decision, the court held that changes to the electoral process "target African Americans with almost surgical precision."

Despite the support of the Supreme Court, many people still oppose voter ID laws. While voter impersonation is possible in theory, there are few recorded cases. There is no evidence impersonation has ever affected the outcome of an election. Meanwhile, millions of Americans do not have photo ID. Some of them, such as elderly voters whose records are not always readily available, cannot easily get a photo ID. Critics of voter ID laws say these very real burdens disenfranchise many people while voter impersonation is an imagined threat.

Felony Disenfranchisement and Racial Injustice

Felony disenfranchisement is another issue that divides the public, even though the Supreme Court has upheld it as well. People convicted of felonies lose their right to vote at least temporarily in forty-eight states. In Maine and Vermont, people convicted of felonies can vote even while serving time in prison. Most states forbid felons from voting in prison and sometimes after release when they are on probation or parole—programs that monitor newly released prisoners, sometimes for years. About a dozen states, however, prevent people convicted of certain crimes from ever casting a ballot again during their lifetime. This is the form of felony disenfranchisement that draws the most criticism.

At the beginning of 2018, about six million Americans could not vote due to felony convictions. This included one in thirteen African Americans and one in fifty-six non-black voters. This racial disparity is also frequently criticized. There is no doubt that felony disenfranchisement was originally used to try to disenfranchise African Americans. It was widely used in the South during Jim Crow. Critics of the practice say that little has changed, and it still affects African Americans far more than other races.

In November 2018, felony disenfranchisement was dealt a serious blow when Florida voters supported a measure to give the right to vote back to all but people convicted of the most serious crimes. In total, 1.5 million Floridians were given the right to vote. Overnight, a quarter of felons who were disenfranchised in the United States regained their ability to cast a ballot.

Today, roughly four and a half million felons cannot vote due to state laws. The issue continues to divide the public. The question of whether crimes should disqualify someone from voting—and for how long—has no easy answer. Meanwhile, nearly as many Americans are disenfranchised because of where they live: overseas American territories. This is a problem that does not always get the same level of attention as other examples of disenfranchisement.

Overseas American Territories

The United States has five inhabited overseas territories: American Samoa, the Northern Mariana Islands, the US Virgin Islands, Guam, and Puerto Rico. People born in these territories are American citizens (except in American Samoa, where they are noncitizen US nationals). In all, more than four million Americans live in an overseas territory.

None of these people, however, can cast a ballot in an American presidential election. This is because it is the electoral college that elects the president, and only states (and Washington, DC) have electors in the electoral college. Overseas territories do not because that is the way the system is defined in the US Constitution.

Most of the four million Americans living in overseas territories live in Puerto Rico. Since they are American citizens, Puerto Ricans can vote in presidential elections if they move to a state or Washington, DC. If they remain in Puerto Rico, they cannot. The same goes for citizens of Guam, the US Virgin Islands, and the Northern Mariana Islands.

Opponents of this system say it amounts to disenfranchisement. They hope that a constitutional amendment will be passed that gives electoral college votes to overseas territories. This is not without precedent. In 1961, the Twenty-Third Amendment gave Washington, DC, electoral votes, in effect, giving Americans living there a voice in the presidential election. Currently, many political groups and ordinary citizens are working to extend the franchise to Americans living in overseas territories. They hope that one day all Americans will have the right to choose the president no matter where they to live in the country.

Puerto Ricans cannot vote for president unless they move to one of the fifty states. Puerto Ricans do vote for state and local representatives. Pictured here is the Puerto Rican capitol building, El Capitolio.

The Electoral College and Disenfranchisement

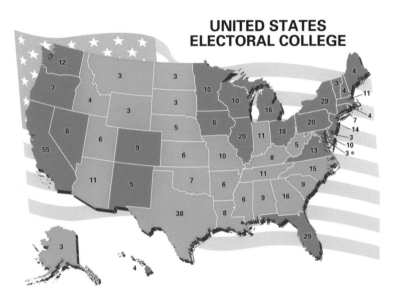

UNITED STATES ELECTORAL COLLEGE

Each state has a particular number of electoral votes, based on its population. This map shows the result of the 2012 presidential race. After the 2020 census, each state's number of votes will change.

When Americans vote for president, the ballot they cast has a complex relationship with the outcome of the election. This is because of the electoral college—a system that is laid out in the Constitution. The person who wins the most Electoral College votes becomes the next president, not the person who wins the most ballots cast by ordinary Americans. This system has led some people to claim that it disenfranchises voters. It is important to recognize that the system does not actually take away people's right to vote, but it may make their votes less valuable than would otherwise be the case.

Each state has a certain number of electoral votes, and the total number of votes is 538. A calculation based on state population decides the exact number of these votes that each state has. The formula favors states with fewer people. In 2016, Wyoming had three electoral votes and Florida had twenty-nine. When this number is compared with the number of people living in the state, it means Wyoming has one vote for every 142,741 people while Florida had one vote for every 510,318 people. In other words, a person's vote in Wyoming was worth more than triple a vote in Florida when it comes to electoral votes, the ones that elect the president.

Another issue with the electoral college is that most states use a winner-take-all approach. This means presidential candidates ignore states that they will win or lose by a large margin. Instead, they campaign in "swing states," like Florida, that have close elections. Critics say that this disenfranchises voters in states that are not swing states.

Whether the electoral college is good or bad is a question that is hotly debated in American politics. The electoral college is responsible for presidents like George W. Bush and Donald Trump losing the popular vote but winning elections. However, it will not change without a constitutional amendment, which is unlikely in the current political climate.

CHAPTER 3

Voting Around the World

D emocracies around the globe handle the right to vote in different ways. Some countries enfranchise more voters than the United States. In many nations, felony disenfranchisement is a thing of the past. Other countries still have problems that the United States no longer confronts. Violence at polling places and other heavy-handed ways of stopping people from voting still occur in some countries.

Canada and the Right to Vote

In Canada, the Canadian Charter of Rights and Freedoms guarantees the right to vote for citizens. Section 3 states, "Every citizen of Canada has the right to vote in an election of members of the House of Commons or of a legislative assembly and to be qualified for membership therein." The Canadian House of Commons is similar to the US Congress. The Canadian prime minister, a position comparable to US president, is a member of the House of Commons.

Opposite: Some countries stain voters' fingers with ink to make sure no one votes more than once. This woman from Guinea displays her ink-stained finger and electoral card.

With the exception of the Chief Electoral Officer and the Assistant Chief Electoral Officer, all Canadians over the age of eighteen have the right to vote for their representative in the House of Commons.

This explicit right to vote in Canada is very different from the law of the United States. The Constitution does not actually state that Americans have a right to vote. It says the right to vote cannot be *taken away* due to race, sex, or age, but it can be taken away on account of past crimes.

Due to Section 3 of the Canadian Charter of Right and Freedoms, many types of disenfranchisement have been struck down in Canada. In the past, people with intellectual disabilities, judges, and some prisoners could not vote. The Canadian Supreme Court, however, overturned all these voting restrictions in accordance with Section 3.

Some groups in the United States are pushing for a similar constitutional amendment in the United States. They hope that an explicit right to vote will help to end different forms of disenfranchisement that still exist.

Prisoners and the Right to Vote

In many countries around the world, prisoners and people convicted of a crime never lose their right to vote. In fact, in more than twenty countries, people serving time in prison can still cast their ballot. For instance, in Germany, prisons are responsible for encouraging prisoners to cast a ballot. In many other countries, only people serving time in prison are prevented from voting. The American system, where some felons lose their right to vote for the rest of their life, is one of the strictest in the world. There are only a handful of democratic countries in the world that disenfranchise felons for life.

Allowing felons to vote is often seen as part of their rehabilitation. People released from prison are less likely to commit crimes in the future if they rejoin society. This includes measures like finding

A prisoner casts a ballot in Israel in 2015.

a job, securing housing, and furthering their education. It also includes voting in elections along with other citizens. There are few acts as symbolically important as casting a vote. Voting is what gives citizens a sense that their government represents them and that they have a voice in their country. This is one reason that many countries allow felons to vote from prison. Voting helps them see themselves as part of a larger society, making it less likely they will commit crimes when they are released.

Nelson Mandela

Even after his death, Nelson Mandela remains one of the world's most respected political figures. Mandela was born in South Africa during apartheid, a system of racial segregation. Depending on the color of their skin, people in South Africa were restricted to living and working in different parts of the country. Black South Africans could not vote and had few rights. Apartheid was even stricter than Jim Crow in the American South.

Mandela worked tirelessly to end apartheid. He recognized that to secure freedom for blacks and end injustice, black South Africans needed to gain the right to vote. In 1961, Mandela appeared on television for the first time and said: "The Africans require, want, the franchise on the basis of one man, one vote. They want political independence." It was a statement that would characterize his political career.

Just a few years later, Mandela was sentenced to life imprisonment for trying to end apartheid, but this did not end his struggle. Behind bars for more than twenty years, he was an inspiration to South Africans fighting for racial equality and freedom. After he was released from prison, the first election where black South Africans could vote was finally held in 1994. Mandela was elected president, and a new era of freedom dawned in South Africa.

Nelson Mandela attends a political rally in 1994, days before he is elected South Africa's first black president.

Violence and Voter Suppression

During Jim Crow, violence was often used in the United States to prevent minorities from voting. African Americans who tried to cast a ballot in some states risked being attacked and even killed. During the civil rights movement, activists working against Jim Crow were likewise targeted. In 1964, three civil rights workers registering African Americans to vote in Mississippi were killed by a lynch mob. Today, such political violence surrounding elections is no longer an issue in the United States, but it remains a problem in other countries.

Police clash with civilians in the tense run-up to the Bangladeshi elections in 2018.

On December 30, 2018, the country of Bangladesh held national elections. Although the country has a history of democratic transfers of power, some critics say the prime minister, Sheikh Hasina, is making the country less democratic. When Bangladeshis voted that day, there was widespread violence at polls across the country. At least twelve people were killed in clashes on election day in many different areas of the country. Opponents of the prime minister reported that they were intimidated and harassed by armed men. Some said they were forced to cast their ballot while representatives from the ruling party watched. As a result, many international observers expressed doubts that the election was truly free and fair.

Bangladesh is not alone in dealing with electoral violence. It is a frequent problem in democracies around the world. Violence can make people too afraid to go to the polls to vote. This makes it impossible to hold an election that reflects the will of the people.

Mandatory Voting

Some countries take voting so seriously that people are required to vote. In more than twenty countries, voting is mandatory. The penalty for not voting is typically light. For example, in Australia, people who do not vote may face a $20 fine.

Compulsory (or mandatory) voting makes sure that many people get out and cast a ballot. In the 2016 elections in Australia, 87 percent of voting-age people cast a ballot. In the same year in the United States, 55.7 percent of voting-age people cast a ballot.

Ensuring that people vote is important in a democracy. The more people who vote for a candidate, the more legitimate the candidate's win appears. In theory, if everyone voted in a race between two candidates, the winner would have the support of

By international standards, U.S. voter turnout is low

Votes cast in most recent national election as a ...

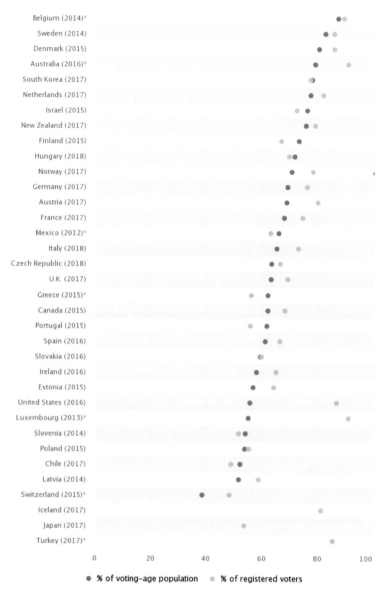

Belgium (2014)*
Sweden (2014)
Denmark (2015)
Australia (2016)*
South Korea (2017)
Netherlands (2017)
Israel (2015)
New Zealand (2017)
Finland (2015)
Hungary (2018)
Norway (2017)
Germany (2017)
Austria (2017)
France (2017)
Mexico (2012)*
Italy (2018)
Czech Republic (2018)
U.K. (2017)
Greece (2015)*
Canada (2015)
Portugal (2015)
Spain (2016)
Slovakia (2016)
Ireland (2016)
Estonia (2015)
United States (2016)
Luxembourg (2013)*
Slovenia (2014)
Poland (2015)
Chile (2017)
Latvia (2014)
Switzerland (2015)*
Iceland (2017)
Japan (2017)
Turkey (2017)*

0   20   40   60   80   100

● % of voting-age population   ● % of registered voters

Note: Voting-age population (VAP) turnout is derived from estimates of each country's VAP by the International Institute for Democracy and Electoral Assistance. Registered-voter (RV) turnout derived from each country's reported registration data. Because of methodology differences, in some countries estimated VAP is lower than reported RV. Current voting-age population estimates for Iceland, Japan and Turkey unavailable.

Voter turnout varies a great deal from country to country. The United States ranks below average.

the majority of voters. However, when very few people vote, the winner may not have much support at all. Donald Trump won the 2016 election with just 27 percent of voting-age Americans voting for him. That number is typical for an American election, where voter turnout is usually between 50 and 60 percent. In countries with compulsory voting, however, it is nearly impossible to win an election with so few votes.

Questions of whether you should have to vote and who should be disenfranchised are extremely important in a democracy. The answers to these questions determine who the government will represent. When many people have their right to vote taken away, the government no longer reflects society. Likewise, if most of the population does not bother to cast a ballot, the government is less likely to reflect the will of the people. Countries around the world seek to answer these questions as best they can for their unique situations.

Women's Suffrage Around the World

Today, women can vote in every democratic country in the world. However, this right was hard-won in many cases and often took years of protest and struggle. In fact, in Saudi Arabia, women just gained the right to vote in local elections in 2015. (National elections are not held in the country since it is a monarchy, ruled by a king, and not a democracy.)

Some countries gave women the right to vote long before the United States did in 1920. New Zealand was one of the first. It allowed women to vote in 1893. Many European nations followed suit in 1918 and 1919 in the aftermath of World War I; new governments that came into existence following the war often extended suffrage to women. For instance, this occurred in Germany, where defeat in the war ended the monarchy, and in Poland, which had not been a country before the war began.

Switzerland was one of the last democracies to allow women to vote. The Swiss government is notable because it is a direct democracy. People cast ballots on actual decisions the government makes rather than to elect representatives. In 1959, a referendum—or people's vote—was held to decide if women should have the right to vote, but 67 percent of males voted "no." Finally, in 1971, a majority of men voted "yes," and women gained the right to vote in Switzerland.

A Saudi woman exercises her right to vote in 2015, the first year that the franchise was extended to women in Saudi Arabia.

CHAPTER 4

The Power of the People

In a democracy, it is the people who hold the power to change the government. While elected representatives make the laws, it is the people who vote in elections and "hire" and "fire" representatives. Often, it is the people protesting, voting, and making their voices heard that inspires great change in a country. Disenfranchisement is no exception. Throughout American and world history, greater voting rights usually resulted from ordinary Americans working together to expand the franchise. It is through the power of the people that the United States has moved closer to the promise of democracy: one person, one vote.

Referendums

Typically, laws in a democracy are passed by elected representatives. Voters rarely get the chance to cast a ballot on a particular issue. Instead, they vote for representatives who broadly share their views but may not agree with them

Opposite: A felon and voting rights activist registers to vote in Florida in 2019 after the state changed its felony disenfranchisement law.

on some issues. Referendums are an exception to this system. In a referendum, the people vote for or against a law or constitutional amendment. In the United States, there are no federal referendums that all Americans can vote on, but many state and local governments do have referendums.

It was a referendum that gave most felons in Florida their right to vote back. In 2018, nearly eight million Floridians voted on the amendment. About 65 percent voted in favor of it. This was not surprising because many Republican and Democratic lawmakers and organizations supported the amendment.

Referendums are one of the most direct ways that an individual can make their voice heard. Typically, a small group of organizers will work to get a referendum on the ballot. This usually requires a certain number of petition signatures from voters. Then, volunteers and organizations will spread the word about the referendum and try to win supporters. If you are very passionate about a cause, you can have a great impact by working to get a referendum passed.

Elected Representatives

When there is no referendum related to disenfranchisement taking place, you can still make a difference by voting for representatives that share your view. Whether you are for or against issues like felony disenfranchisement and voter ID laws, there are likely politicians who agree with you. In addition to voting, you can volunteer for a candidate's campaign or donate money. This kind of support is what allows candidates to spread their message and improve their chances of winning.

Even if the candidate you supported was not elected, you can still make your views known. Contacting your representative by phone, mail, or email lets them know what your opinion is on an

Supporters of Senator Ted Cruz make phone calls on his behalf. Volunteers play a crucial role in election campaigns.

issue. Since most voters do not feel strongly enough about an issue to go through this effort, your one letter or phone call speaks for many people. If a representative receives a dozen letters about an issue, they know many more people likely feel the same way.

How Old Should Voters Be?

For much of American history, only people twenty-one years of age or older could vote. This began to change in 1960s when the United States was fighting in the Vietnam War, and young men between the ages of eighteen and twenty were responsible for much of the fighting. More than half of the American servicemen who died in the war were not yet twenty-one years old. It seemed unjust that people dying for their country could not legally vote.

In 1971, the Twenty-Sixth Amendment to the Constitution was ratified. It guaranteed that no one over the age of eighteen could have their right to vote restricted on account of their age. In effect, it changed the minimum voting age to eighteen.

Today, there is a small movement in the United States to change the minimum voting age to sixteen rather than eighteen. Supporters say this will engage younger Americans in the political process. Many sixteen- and seventeen-year-olds say that they deserve a voice: they know about current issues, and problems like gun violence can affect them directly.

So far, some American cities have lowered the voting age to sixteen for local elections. Washington, DC, considered a law to lower the voting age to sixteen in November 2018, but eventually it was dropped. It remains to be seen if more cities or states will move forward with lowering the voting age in the future.

A US Army general speaks to an eighteen-year-old soldier during the Vietnam War. For much of the Vietnam War, the voting age was twenty-one, and many young soldiers who gave their lives never had the opportunity to vote.

Protests

Aside from participating in referendums and political campaigns, there are other ways you can inspire change. Large-scale protests are one means that activists have used for many years to spur the government into action. When women were campaigning for the right to vote, they often marched through the streets holding signs. Likewise, during the civil rights movement, African Americans and their allies marched to end Jim Crow and disenfranchisement. Dr. Martin Luther King Jr.'s March on Washington is just one example of many. It inspired hundreds of thousands of people to gather in Washington, DC, to protest racial injustice. Dr. King delivered his famous "I Have a Dream" speech before the crowd.

Today, individuals and groups still march and protest about issues that are important to them. This includes issues like felony disenfranchisement and voting restriction laws. Taking part in a peaceful protest or march lets politicians know that many people care about an issue.

The March on Washington, led by Dr. Martin Luther King Jr., was a pivotal moment in the civil rights movement.

Staying Informed

It is important to keep reading and learning about current issues like disenfranchisement. Voter ID laws, voting restrictions, and felony disenfranchisement laws can change quite rapidly. States pass new laws regularly, and the courts sometimes overturn old laws. These critical issues are always evolving.

When you read more about disenfranchisement, you need to keep in mind the source of that information. Voting restrictions like voter ID laws are a partisan issue in the United States, meaning that the two major political parties, the Democrats and Republicans, see the issue quite differently. Typically, Republicans tend to support voter ID laws and some other voting restrictions. Democrats usually oppose them. As a result, news articles may report on a voter ID law very differently depending on whether they lean Democratic or Republican.

The best way to combat partisan news sources is to keep an open mind and read broadly. If two articles cover the same topic very differently, look at their arguments. See if they give good reasons for their position and if they have evidence to back up their claims. You may need to think critically and research more to come to your own conclusion. Staying informed is not always easy, but it is the responsibility of every citizen in a democracy.

Reading a variety of newspapers or online news sources lets you see both sides of a debate.

The Black Lives Matter movement advocates for many issues, including voting rights.

Supporting Organizations

As an individual, you can vote in a referendum, contact your representative, or publicly protest an issue. Your voice, however, is just one of many. To increase the odds that your opinion is heard and respected, you can work with an organization of like-minded citizens. When many people band together, they can work more effectively on an issue.

If you care about disenfranchisement, there are many organizations that you can join or support that share your concerns. Some of these organizations are focused on a single issue: disenfranchisement or the rights of people convicted of crimes. For example, the Florida Rights Restoration Coalition is a group that worked to end lifetime felony disenfranchisement in Florida. Many Floridians who shared the same views on the issue came together to form that group. Other organizations and movements, like the American Civil Liberties Union (ACLU) and Black Lives Matter, focus on many related issues. The ACLU works to protect civil rights for Americans across the country. In 2018, this included campaigning in Florida to end felony disenfranchisement. Black Lives Matter works to tackle racial injustices of all kinds.

Disenfranchisement Today

Right now, disenfranchisement is a topic that is sparking debates across the United States. Questions about when felons should be able to vote and whether Americans living in overseas territories should vote for the president are in the news regularly. Uncertainty about voter ID laws and other new voting restrictions have raised concerns about both voter fraud and voter disenfranchisement. The ugly history of Jim Crow makes these issues especially sensitive.

It is the responsibility of all Americans to take these issues seriously and try to work together to come to a solution. Once you have examined an issue and formed your own views, it is crucial that you make your voice heard. This is how change occurs in a democracy. By staying informed and speaking up, you can influence the laws that govern who can and cannot vote.

GLOSSARY

amendment A change or addition to a law or constitution. In the United States, constitutional amendments have often been extremely important to history. For example, the Thirteenth Amendment banned slavery.

ballot A piece of paper on which voters indicate who or what they are voting for.

disenfranchise To take away someone's right to vote.

divisive An issue that causes widespread disagreement.

federal Relating to the federal government in Washington, DC, that governs the whole of the United States. State and local governments are separate from the federal government.

felony A crime that is more serious than lesser offenses, which are known as "misdemeanors." Examples of felonies include possession of some drugs, some kinds of theft, and violent crimes.

franchise The right to vote.

Jim Crow A name for the era of racial discrimination in the South that took place between 1877 and the mid-1960s. Schools and other public services were divided by race. African Americans were also systematically disenfranchised.

poll tax Money that must be paid before someone can cast their vote.

precinct A voting district.

predetermined Decided in advance.

referendum A direct vote by the people on an issue.

Shelby County v. Holder The landmark 2013 Supreme Court decision that overturned part of the Voting Rights Act. As a result of this decision, many states passed new voting restriction laws.

suffrage The right to vote.

unconstitutional Contradicting the constitution; if a court declares a law or practice unconstitutional, the government must stop doing it.

voter fraud When votes are cast illegally by someone who does not have the right to vote or when someone votes more than once.

voter suppression The mass disenfranchisement of a group or groups of people, often to affect the outcome of an election.

FURTHER INFORMATION

Books

Fremon, David K. *The Jim Crow Laws and Racism in United States History*. New York: Enslow Publishers, 2014.

Quinlan, Julia J. *Everything You Need to Know About Voting Rights and Voter Disenfranchisement*. New York: Rosen Publishing Group, 2018.

Websites

Criminal Disenfranchisement Laws Across the United States

https://www.brennancenter.org/criminal-disenfranchisement-laws-across-united-states

The Brennan Center spotlights how each state treats the voting rights of people convicted of a felony.

The Sentencing Project: Felony Disenfranchisement

https://www.sentencingproject.org/issues/felony-disenfranchisement/

An organization that promotes criminal justice reform presents facts and reports about felony disenfranchisement in the United States.

Voter ID Restrictions Imposed since 2010

https://www.aclu.org/issues/voting-rights/fighting-voter-suppression/voter-id-restrictions-imposed-2010

The ACLU provides a map that shows which states have recently passed voter ID laws as well as the details of those laws.

Videos

Florida Voter Disenfranchisement: Demetrius Jifunza

https://www.youtube.com/watch?v=u7yepMwbgL0

PBS NewsHour hears from a man who was disenfranchised for life in Florida after being convicted of a crime.

Wisconsin Voter ID Law Has Students, Homeless Jumping Through Hoops

https://www.youtube.com/watch?v=bu_-JnrpQbo

MSNBC examines Wisconsin's voter ID law and interviews people affected by it.

BIBLIOGRAPHY

Arnsdorf, Isaac. "These Voters Had to Wait for Hours: 'It Felt Like a Type of Disenfranchisement.'" *ProPublica*, November 6, 2018. https://www.propublica.org/article/these-voters-had-to-wait-for-hours-it-felt-like-a-type-of-disenfranchisement.

Astor, Maggie. "Seven Ways Alabama Has Made It Harder to Vote." *New York Times*, June 23, 2018. https://www.nytimes.com/2018/06/23/us/politics/voting-rights-alabama.html.

Cassidy, Christina A., and Ivan Morena. "Voter ID Law Proved Insurmountable for Many in Wisconsin." *Wisconsin State Journal*, May 9, 2017. https://madison.com/wsj/news/local/govt-and-politics/voter-id-law-proved-insurmountable-for-many-in-wisconsin/article_408d1ad4-33cb-56aa-9635-45f6699c4af5.html.

Crews, Ed. "Voting in Early America." Colonial Williamsburg, 2007. http://www.history.org/foundation/journal/spring07/elections.cfm.

Domonoske, Camila. "US Appeals Court Strikes Down North Carolina's Voter ID Law." *NPR*, July 29, 2016. https://www.npr.org/sections/thetwo-way/2016/07/29/487935700/u-s-appeals-court-strikes-down-north-carolinas-voter-id-law.

Kirk, Chris. "How Powerful Is Your Vote?" *Slate*, November 2, 2012. http://www.history.org/foundation/journal/spring07/elections.cfm.

Lopez, German. "Supreme Court's Conservative Justices Uphold Ohio's Voter Purge System." Vox, June 1, 2018. https://www.vox.com/policy-and-politics/2018/6/11/17448742/ohio-voter-purge-supreme-court-ruling.

Moreau, Julie. "Strict ID Laws Could Disenfranchise 78,000 Transgender Voters, Report Says." *NBC News*, August 17, 2018. https://www.nbcnews.com/feature/nbc-out/strict-id-laws-could-disenfranchise-78-000-transgender-voters-report-n901696.

Niesse, Mark, Maya T. Prabhu, and Jacquelyn Elias. "Voting Precincts Closed Across Georgia since Election Oversight Lifted." *Atlanta-Journal Constitution*, August 31, 2018. https://www.ajc.com/news/state--regional-govt--politics/voting-precincts-closed-across-georgia-since-election-oversight-lifted/bBkHxptlim0Gp9pKu7dfrN.

Raskin, Jamin. "Lawful Disenfranchisement: America's Structural Democracy Deficit." American Bar Association, March 23, 2012. https://www.americanbar.org/publications/human_rights_magazine_home/human_rights_vol32_2005/spring2005/hr_spring05_lawful.

INDEX

ABOUT THE AUTHOR

Derek Miller is a writer and educator from Salisbury, Maryland. He is the author of more than a dozen books for middle school and high school students, including *Dilemmas in Democracy: Military Force* and *Dilemmas in Democracy: Money in Politics*. In his free time, Miller enjoys reading and traveling with his wife.